Ride the Nightmare

Ride the Nightmare

verse and prose by

Adrian Mitchell

JONATHAN CAPE
THIRTY BEDFORD SQUARE, LONDON

THIS COLLECTION FIRST PUBLISHED 1971

© 1971 BY ADRIAN MITCHELL

JONATHAN CAPE LTD
30 BEDFORD SQUARE, LONDON WC1

ISBN 0 224 00511 1

PRINTED AND BOUND IN GREAT BRITAIN BY
LEWIS REPRINTS LIMITED, PORT TALBOT, GLAMORGAN

NOTE TO EXAMINERS, CHILDREN AND STUDENTS

None of the work in this or any other
of my books or articles is to be used
in connection with any examination
whatsoever. This also applies to
beauty contests.

This book is dedicated to my
friends and allies.

ACKNOWLEDGMENTS

This collection includes verse, articles and other pieces which have appeared in *The Black Dwarf, C'Mon Everybody, Evening Standard, How It Is, The Lesser Known Shag, The Listener, Night Ride, Oclae* (Cuba), *Peace News* and *Viva Che.*

There are three poems from my commentary for Roy Battersby's film *The Body* (Kestrel Films). There are song lyrics from the University of Lancaster's Song Workshop productions of *The Hotpot Saga* (a black pantomime about a race war between Lancashire and Yorkshire) and *Lash Me To The Mast!* (a musical version of the *Odyssey*). There are also extracts from *Move Over, Jehovah* or *The Man Who Shot Emily Brontë,* a dramatization of the Old Testament produced by Albert Hunt for the National Association for Mental Health.

CONTENTS

VROOMPH! or THE POPULAR ELASTIC WAIST

(A cut-up of sentences from the *Sunday Times* Colour Magazine
of December 9th, 1967, which featured Civil Defence, Famous
Footballers, The Girls of Thailand, Gangsters and several
advertisements.)

Juliet sighs. Romeo speaks.
Deep shelters are out of most people's reach.
The white tin is a simple gadget for pinpointing
    the size and position of nuclear bursts.
Simply push the needle in, pump the handle, and
You haven't seen anything till you've seen
    the 200 pounds of beautiful Louise
Tucked away in the secret, hardened, national seat
    of government,
Or balanced on bicycles while removing 12 shirts.
Yet, even when we made love, at a time when most
    women are feeling romantic, she would start to
      prattle away about
The Royal State Trumpeters of the Household Cavalry.

Stimulated by these breaks in the nuclear overcast,
    the *Sunday Times* here offers what is probably the
      first complete review of our Civil Defence
        preparations,
A symbol of the virile, aggressive, muscular game which
    one associates with a man who has twice broken the
      same leg — and twice returned to the game.
This is the problem: whether to drink Cointreau neat
    and slowly savour every warming sip,
Or hang from the tops of palm trees by our feet.

While we have the bomb it seems ridiculous not to be honest.
It works like this: the motor is powered by ordinary
    torch batteries.
The slightly wounded will be sent on their way, the
    severely wounded left to
The Marquis de Ferara.

1

Fill out the Panic Sheet.
Neither the *Sunday Times* nor its agents accepts any
      liability for loss or
The gruesome electric chair.
You see, we are unashamedly devoted to the kind
      of quiet courtesy
          which gets rarer
            every
              day.

TO A RUSSIAN SOLDIER IN PRAGUE

You are going to be hated by the people.

They will hate you over their freakish breakfast of tripe soup and
                                                            pastries.
They will squint hatred at you on their way to pretend to work.
By the light of yellow beer they will hate you with jokes you'll
                                                        never hear.

You're beginning to feel
Like a landlord in a slum
Like a white man in Harlem
Like a U.S. Marine in Saigon

Socialists are hated
By all who kill for profit and power.
But you are going to be hated by
The people — who are all different.
The people — who are all extraordinary.
The people — who are all of equal value.
Socialism is theirs, it was invented for them.
Socialism is theirs, it can only be made by them.

Africa, Asia and Latin America are screaming:
STARVATION. POVERTY. OPPRESSION.
When they turn to America
They see only flames and children in the flames.
When they turn to England
They see an old lady in a golden wheelchair,
Share certificates in one hand, a pistol in the other.
When they turn to Russia
They see — you.

You are going to be hated
As the English have usually been hated.
The starving, the poor and the oppressed
Are turning, turning away.
While you nervously guard a heap of documents

They stagger away through the global crossfire
Towards revolution, towards socialism.

FLAG DAY — BUT NOT FOR THE REVOLUTION

Hunger scrapes the inside out of the human belly.
Your charity small change clanks into the tin
And makes no real change.
They are not slot machines for your spare pennies
Although you can read your own gross weight
Scrawled across their faces.
The razors of hunger slash and slash and slash their skin
And all your fat pity helps no one but yourself.

WHAT TO DO IF YOU MEET NIJINSKY

The special child
Remains a child
Knowing that everything else
Is smaller, meaner and less gentle.

Watch the creature standing
Like a fountain in a photograph.
He's moving carefully as a leaf
Growing in a hothouse.
What are the roots?
What is the stem?
What are the flowers?
Nijinsky
Dancing too much truth.

If you don't kill Nijinsky
He's going to turn you into Nijinsky.
You'll live like a leaf, die like a leaf,
Like Nijinsky.

Sweet magical
Skinned
Alive
Animal

You must decide for yourself how you're going to kill Nijinsky.

Leave him in the prison
Whose stones are cut so cleverly
They fit every contour of his skin exactly.

Leave him collapsing
In the foreign forest clearing
While the pine trees burn around him like a circle
of matches.

Climb into your car and drive like a rocket right out of the world
of feeling.

6

Leave Nijinsky dancing
The dance of lying very still.

FAMILY PLANNING

Why do the Spanish have so many children?

Our first child was a priest.
Then we had a nun.
The next three were all policemen.

You've got to have one child you can talk to.

WOULD YOU MIND SIGNING THIS RECEIPT?

When you get back home
You will find a black patch on the ground,
A patch of blackness shaped like a house
Where your house used to stand.

It was a mistake.
It was the wrong house.
It was all a mistake
Based on faulty information.

When you get back home
You will find three black heaps on the ground.
Three black heaps shaped like children
On the patch of blackness shaped like a house
Where your house used to stand.

It was a mistake.
They were the wrong people.
It was all a mistake
Based on faulty information.

Three children.
51 dollars compensation per child.
That comes to 153 dollars, madam.

UNDER PHOTOGRAPHS OF TWO PARTY LEADERS, SMILING

These two smiled so the photographer
Could record their smiles
FOR YOU

As they smiled these smiles
They were thinking all the time
OF YOU

They smile on the rich
They smile on the poor
They smile on the victim in his village
They smile on the killer in his cockpit

Yes, Mummy and Daddy
Are smiling, smiling
AT YOU

please try to smile back.

HUNGRY SONG (from *Lash Me To The Mast!*)

Anchovies in aspic
With marinated aubergines.
Beetroot bellies in brandy
With a bucket of Heinz Baked Beans.
Alligator purée and I don't care
If you serve it with bacon rind,
But gastronomic pornography
Is booting me out of my mind.

Caviar and cake mix
Makes coriander chocolate cheese.
Chutneyed carrots and coffee —
Won't you slice me a doorstep please?
Pass me down a mousse with its antlers on
You can cook it in Fairy Snow,
For gastronomic pornography
Is dragging me down so low.

Gammon stuffed with garlic,
Geraniums and gooseberry fool.
Grouse, gazpacho and ginger,
Burn your kitchen and leave to cool.
I want Mrs Beeton to be my man
And Elizabeth David too,
For gastronomic pornography
Makes my stomach feel like a zoo.

TV TALK

I thought it was about time we had a little chat. You know Charlie,
he hates pity. People who need people are the luckiest people in
the world. We have seen chaos and confusion, if I may use that
expression. I think we've got to rely on the decency and fair play
of Rhodesians. I saw something from Heaven that made the sun
look dim. There must be something else we can talk about, yes,
prisons. It's his whole life, the game and what goes with it. Once
you get beyond the Green Belt you may as well be in Timbuctoo.
You're playing a very dangerous game, Delia. He's a rum bloke,
that Mr Dodgson. Nobody's indispensable — nobody. Koala
means: 'He does not drink. He really does not drink.' Sex is the
mysticism of materialism. Let's get down the building site and
cause a bit of damage. The pursuit of the goal must be unre-
mitting and continuous. Coffee with Life In It. I have no
aspirations in that area. Breakfast is an essential meal of which
eggs are an essential part. If twenty ministers of the Church
decided to go on the rampage, they could do just as much
damage as twenty teenagers. Each one of the commercials is
going to be a little parable. Well, how about that one, pop-
pickers? We order our news editors to be objective. Getting
married started when we went to look at furniture. Probably,
like most other abuses, it's less than it seems. He's like a man
in a trance — I don't think he's known much about it for the
last four rounds. The still primitive passions of the people are
mirrored in their faces. Few as one's readers may be, at least
one knows they can read. Down every street there are folks
like you and I. Yes, if it's limited to twenty megadeaths, we
can accept that. Well there you are ladies, you can get another
pair of curtains washed tomorrow . . .

OPEN DAY AT PORTON

These bottles are being filled with madness,
A kind of liquid madness concentrate
Which can be drooled across the land
Leaving behind a shuddering human highway . . .

    A welder trying to eat his arm.

    Children pushing stale food into their eyes
    To try to stop the chemical spectaculars
    Pulsating inside their hardening skulls.

    A health visitor throwing herself downstairs,
    Climbing the stairs, throwing herself down again
    Shouting: Take the nails out of my head.

There is no damage to property.

Now, nobody likes manufacturing madness,
But if we didn't make madness in bottles
We wouldn't know how to deal with bottled madness.

We don't know how to deal with bottled madness.

We all really hate manufacturing madness
But if we didn't make madness in bottles
We wouldn't know how to be sane.

Responsible madness experts assure us
Britain would never be the first
To uncork such a global brainquake.

But suppose some foreign nut sprayed Kent
With his insanity aerosol . . .
Well, there's only one answer to madness.

INCIDENT

At Chorley Station on May 30th, 1969, I saw a railwayman
bailing out the signal-box with a pewter mug and pouring
the water inaccurately down into a scarlet wheelbarrow.

MAXIMUM SECURITY GIRL (from *The Hotpot Saga*)

Some girls are searching for marzipan visions
Some of them want nothing but eternal laughter
Some want a surgeon to make their decisions
But this girl knows exactly what she's after —

She wants a town that has no people
So she's never in a crowd
She wants a town that has no people
Where strangers aren't allowed
She wants the countryside disinfected
So that stinging nettles won't grow
And a maximum security prison
For everyone she doesn't know

Then she'll be safe
That's what she said
Safer than insurance
Safer than the dead
She wants to be the safest person
In this dangerous dangerous world
Maximum security girl

She wants a house that has no windows
So the sun can't hurt her skin
She wants a house that has no windows
So the neighbours can't look in
She wants a maximum security garden
With land-mines planted in the ground
And a hundred and one alsatians
And electric fences all around

Then she'll have peace
That's what she said
Safer than insurance
Safer than the dead
She wants to be the safest person
In this dangerous dangerous world
Maximum security girl

THE BALLAD OF THE DEATH OF AESCHYLUS

Eagle flying along
hey hey
Eagle flying along
Swinging his golden all along the hey hey sky

Tortoise rumbling along
hey hey
Tortoise rumbling along
Dreaming of salad if you want the hey hey truth

But that was one heap of an
Astigmatic eagle
Astigmatic eagle
The kind of person
Who looks at a tortoise
And believes he's seeing casserole

Eagle swivelling down
hey hey
Eagle swivelling down
Clamping that tortoise into his beak
Dragging him up into a neighbouring cloud
And shutting the hey hey door

    Aeschylus was steaming through Athens
    Somewhere near the Parthenon Gents
    It is believed
    Aeschylus was steaming through Athens
    Out to get his tragical propens-
    ities relieved

That's the hey hey set up so remember it love
Man down below and an eagle plus a tortoise up above
Better carve that message in a durable cheese
And let it learn you a bit of manners please

It wasn't one of your charter flights
The eagle got Aeschylus in his sights

16

It was tortoise away and super-zap
Doing kerflumph and possibly BAP
Does anyone want a flat-headed tragedian?

Poor old bloody Aeschylus
hey hey
Poor old bloody Aeschylus
Come to that poor old bloody tortoise

HOW TO KILL CUBA

You must burn the people first,
Then the grass and trees, then the stones.
You must cut the island out of all the maps,
The history books, out of the old newspapers,
Even the newspapers which hated Cuba,
And burn all these, and burn
The paintings, poems and photographs and films
And when you have burnt all these
You must bury the ashes
You must guard the grave
And even then
Cuba will only be dead like Che Guevara —
Technically dead, that's all,
Technically dead.

THE DEATH OF NOAH (from *Move Over, Jehovah*)

(NOAH is on his bed, dying.
Around him his dead friends, in mud-coloured clothes, form a sea
which heaves and eventually rises to cover him.
NOAH's son SHEM stands in front of the bed.)

SHEM

I have seen a lot of people die. But this is how my father, Noah,
died. He was old. Sometimes his head was as hot as fire. Sometimes
it was like very cold water. When he called for wine, we gave it to
him. Most of the time he thought he was back on the Ark and the
waters were rising. He wasn't talking to us. He was talking to the
people drowning all around the Ark.

(A face emerges from the sea, a man.)

FIRST DROWNING MAN

Noah. Last summer. We used to drink together. Let me into the
Ark.

NOAH

God says the earth is corrupt. But I found grace in the eyes of
the Lord.

FIRST DROWNING WOMAN

Noah. I taught your sons to sing. Let me in.

NOAH

God says the earth is filled with violence. But I found grace in the
eyes of the Lord.

SECOND DROWNING WOMAN

Noah. Your wife screamed. You cried. I was there. I delivered your
sons. Let me into the Ark.

NOAH

God says he is sorry he made man. But I found grace in the eyes of
the Lord.

SECOND DROWNING MAN (CLUTCHING WITH ONE ARM THIRD DROWNING WOMAN)
Noah. She's pregnant. Let her in.

(NOAH sits up, straining against the bedclothes as if tied by ropes.)

NOAH

There's no room. I've seen a lot of people drowning, and they all
drown differently. Some call out their own names. Some call out
other names. Some clutch on to barrels or branches and float for
a time, but they all go down in the end. They have to let go, the
water is so bad to them.
A friend of mine spat at me just before I drowned. I mean, just
before he drowned.
The sky is the same colour as the flood.
The flood is the same colour as the sky.
There is nothing else.
Perhaps the sky is reflecting the flood and the flood is reflecting
the sky.
They are both the same colour as death.
The flood is mad. And the sky. They're both the same.
But I found grace in the eyes of the Lord.
His eyes are the same colour as the flood.
I wish he had looked for someone else. My head is full of rain.
I don't want to go into the Ark.
I'll stay with my friends. I want to stay with my friends.
I want to be wiped out.

(The sea rises and covers NOAH.)

SHEM

We kept giving him wine. We gave him too much wine — on pur-
pose. His head was full of voices screaming at him. We took turns
being with him. After lunch, I went up to see him for a few
minutes. I told him there was nothing to worry about. He said,
It's awful, and I asked if there was anything I could do. He asked
if I would draw the curtains so it would be darker. I drew the
curtains.

20

WE MOVED TO A FARMHOUSE IN THE YORKSHIRE DALES
AND LOOK WHAT HAPPENED

Let your soul roll around these horizons,
An unchipped marble with clouds inside
Buzzing around the huge green bowl of meadows.

We sleepwalk, musically, down the tunnels of this grey rock
Which was excavated by a painstaking Jacobean drunk
Who hewed out slit-eyed bedrooms and the largest bathroom in
the world.

It all looks as easy as the pink felt pig
Which lies so sideways between the upended Czech projection
screen
And the solid leather suitcase which holds no more than a
monochrome postcard.

It all looks gigantic as our first washing machine
Which shakes the landscape, whose brand-name is Jehovah.
This morning, out of its dirty-water gut, the machine produced

A synthesis of Marx Freud Blake Dylan Us in two hundred words,
A small creature, like a golden dog but the size of an ant
And a shower of what I thought at first were hundreds and
thousands

But which hurtled towards the outstretched window
In the direction of the ionosphere. I caught one of them,
Held it for a fifteenth of a second before it burned its way through

The palm of my hand, between the finger bones, and up up and
away.
It was, I noted, a miniature planet
Called Grain or Groin or Groan or something like that

And I saw, in that fleck of a moment, before it joined the flock
Of other confectionary planets, all the creatures on its surface
And they were, you know, they were like we want to be.

And then the speck-size planet flared away from me

And it rolled, like a soul, around these horizons,
An unchipped marble with clouds inside,
Buzzing around this huge green bowl of meadows.

MY UNCLE SUPERHUBERT

My Uncle Superhubert's got no money, no sense, no heart, no
                                                    hope.
But there's one thing everybody's got to admit, my Uncle
                                        Superhubert can cope.

Take the other week.

While the British Government was deciding whether to arm the
        white South Africans for purely economic reasons,
My Uncle closed the export gap by touring Rhodesia wearing only
        postage stamps commemorating the fiftieth birthday of the
                                        Soviet Secret Police.
When Uncle Superhubert heard about Otis Redding's death
He used Cliff Richard's halo to strangle Val Doonican's dentist.
When the newspapers announced that there was a split in the
                                            Liberal Party
He took out an after-life subscription to the *News Chronicle* and
        laid snowballs on Gladstone's grave,
And when the bookies started taking bets on foot-and-mouth
                                            disease
My Uncle ran down to the Stock Exchange and bought a
        controlling interest in leprosy.

No money, no sense, no heart, no hope —
But my Uncle Superhubert can cope.

PLEASE KEEP OFF THE DEAD

My Uncle Superhubert joined the Graveyard Police,
Says you couldn't wish for a sweeter manor.

Sometimes they hold a March of the Zombies,
But that's traditional, my Uncle leads them
Once round the boneyard and back to bed.

He gets the odd villain.
A couple of revolutionaries
Whose graves keep catching on fire
But mostly they're a decent mob, the dead.

Last week my Uncle went down to Gethsemane **Corner**
And rolled the stone away
And there was Bing Crosby
Singing 'The Bells of St Mary's'.

GASTON THE PEASANT

Gaston liked being a peasant. He enjoyed all the things which peasants usually like, elemental things like being born, living and, something he looked forward to with oafish optimism, dying. Often, seated on a sack of blackened truffles in the steam of the peat fire, he would speak of these things:

'We peasants are almost excessively privileged,' he would vouch, in the expressive dialect of the Basques, 'in that not only do we delight in the elemental joys of Mankind, but also in that we are denied the manifold responsibilities accorded will-he nill-he to the holder of high office.'

Gaston had lived a long time, seen much, known many, done little. He was sketched eating turnips by Van Gogh. D.H. Lawrence dropped in to talk to him about the blood. He once tried to cheer up Emile Zola. Orwell slept with his pigs for the experience. Ernest Hemingway borrowed his pitchfork. He did not return. He did not return the pitchfork.

OLD AGE REPORT

When a man's too ill or old to work
We punish him.
Half his income is taken away
Or all of it vanishes and he gets pocket-money.

We should reward these tough old humans for surviving,
Not with a manager's soggy handshake
Or a medal shaped like an alarm clock —
No, make them a bit rich,
Give the freedom they always heard about
When the bloody chips were down
And the blitz or the desert
Swallowed their friends.

Retire, retire into a fungus basement
Where nothing moves except the draught
And the light and dark grey figures
Doubling their money on the screen;
Where the cabbages taste like the mummy's hand
And the meat tastes of feet;
Where there is nothing to say except:
'Remember?' or 'Your turn to dust the cat.'

To hell with retiring. Let them advance.
Give them the money they've always earned
Or more — and let them choose.
If Mr Burley wants to be a miser,
Great, let the moneybags sway and clink for him,
Pay him a pillowful of best doubloons.
So Mrs Wells has always longed to travel?
Print her a season ticket to the universe,
Let her slum-white skin
Be tanned by a dozen different planets.
We could wipe away some of their worry,
Some of their pain — what I mean
Is so bloody simple:
The old people are being robbed

And punished and we ought
To be letting them out of their cages
Into green spaces of enchanting light.

LULLABY TO BE SUNG BY THE MOTHER OF MOSES WHEN SHE LEAVES HIM IN THE BULRUSHES

(From *Move Over, Jehovah,* written in
collaboration with Sasha Mitchell)

There's nothing I can give you any more,
Except a quiet game for playing.
I took a gourd and dried it in the sun,
I hollowed it while you were sleeping.
I filled the gourd with silver desert sand
So you could make it whisper with your hand.
Now it makes a soft sound, a soft sound,
Nobody could hear except a baby.

PRESS PHOTOGRAPHS

Postage Stamp Exhibition

Outside the Central Hall, Westminster,
the Lord Privy Seal releases a carrier pigeon
carrying a message of goodwill
to the Queen as a fellow stamp collector
to celebrate the fiftieth anniversary
of the Tasmanian Pigeon Post.

An old lady with a face of driftwood
clutches the elbow of the Lord Privy Seal.
She tells him that she remembers
the Tasmanian Pigeon Post.

Podola

The day the cops got Podola.
In the wash-room a sub-editor says,
'He'll be getting a good going-over.'
Two sub-editors laugh
as they wash their hands with liquid soap
which smells of vomit.

Pat Boone

I am walking to interview Pat Boone
the Christian crooner
who would rather be dead
and his children dead and everything dead
than red.
I am thinking about Pat Boone
when a tree falls across the road with a long groan
and crushes my shadow.

Phone Call

I ring up an M.P. to ask about her illness.
She says she has cancer.

I tell her I am sorry.
She sounds as if she is smiling.
I tell her I am very sorry.

JUST OFF CHARING CROSS ROAD THERE ARE
ALLEYS FULL OF CROCODILES

I'm dreaming about the fiscal year,
But I promise you, I promise you —
And I'll sharpen my forefinger to
A red-streaming ballpoint pen
So I can put this promise in writing you'll believe —
I don't want to live with Julie Andrews.

Warming my eyes in a bar.
The man on my left says Safe Deposit.
The lady on my right says Shirt.
Someone else says: You'd Think You'd
Get A Decent Life For A Pound A Head.

THE OXFORD HYSTERIA OF ENGLISH POETRY

Back in the caveman days business was fair.
Used to turn up at Wookey Hole,
Plenty of action down the Hole
Nights when it wasn't raided.
They'd see my bear-gut harp
And the mess at the back of my eyes
And 'Right,' they'd say, 'make poetry,'
So I'd slam away at the three basic chords
And go into the act —
A story about sabre-toothed tigers with a comic hero,
A sexy one with an anti-wife-clubbing twist —
Good progressive stuff mainly,
Get ready for the Bronze Age, all that,
And soon it would be 'Bring out the woad!'
Yeah, woad. We used to get high on woad.

The Vikings only wanted sagas
Full of gigantic deadheads cutting off each other's vitals
Or Beowulf Versus the Bog People.
The Romans weren't much better,
Under all that armour you could tell they were soft
With their central heating
And poets with names like Horace.

Under the Normans the language began to clear,
Became a pleasure to write in,
Yes, write in, by now everyone was starting
To write down poems.
Well, it saved memorizing and improvizing
And the peasants couldn't get hold of it.
Soon there were hundreds of us,
Most of us writing under the name
Of Geoffrey Chaucer.

Then suddenly we were knee-deep in sonnets.
Holinshed ran a headline:
BONANZA FOR BARDS.

It got fantastic —
Looning around from the bear-pit to the Globe,
All those freak-outs down the Mermaid,
Kit Marlowe coming on like Richard the Two,
A virgin Queen in a ginger wig
And English poetry in full whatsit —
Bloody fantastic, but I never found any time
To do any writing till Willy finally flipped —
Smoking too much of the special stuff
Sir Walter Raleigh was pushing.

Cromwell's time I spent on cultural committees.

Then Charles the Second swung down from the trees
And it was sexual medley time
And the only verses they wanted
Were epigrams on Chloë's breasts
But I only got published on the back of her left knee-cap.

Next came Pope and Dryden
So I went underground.
Don't mess with the Mafia.

Then suddenly — WOOMF —
It was the Ro-man-tic Re-viv-al
And it didn't matter how you wrote,
All the public wanted was a hairy great image.
Before they'd even print you
You had to smoke opium, die of consumption,
Fall in love with your sister
Or drown in the Mediterranean (not at Brighton).
My publisher said: 'I'll have to remainder you
Unless you go and live in a lake or something
Like this bloke Wordsworth.'

After that there were about
A thousand years of Tennyson
Who got so bored with himself
That he changed his name
To Kipling at half-time.

Strange that Tennyson should be
Remembered for his poems really,
We always thought of him
As a golfer.

There hasn't been much time
For poetry since the 'twenties
What with leaving the Communist Church
To join the Catholic Party
And explaining why in the C.I.A. Monthly.
Finally I was given the Chair of Comparitive Ambiguity
At Armpit University, Java.
It didn't keep me busy,
But it kept me quiet.
It seemed like poetry had been safely tucked up for the night.

AUTOBAHNMOTORWAYAUTOROUTE

Around the gleaming map of Europe
A gigantic wedding ring
Slowly revolves through Londonoslowestberlin
Athensromemadridparis and home again,
Slowly revolving.

That's no ring,
It's the Great European Limousine,
The Famous Goldenwhite Circular Car

Slowly revolving

All the cars in Europe have been welded together
Into a mortal unity,
A roundaboutgrandtourroundabout
Trafficjamroundaboutagain,
All the cars melted together,
Citroenjaguarbugattivolkswagenporschedaf.

Each passenger, lugging his
Colourpiano, frozenmagazines, high-fidog,
Clambers over the seat in front of him
Towards what looks like the front of the car.
They are dragging behind them
Worksofart, lampshades made of human money,
Instant children and exploding clocks.

But the car's a circle
No front no back
No driver no steering wheel no windscreen no brakes no

NAMING THE DEAD

And now the super-powers, who have been cheerfully doubling their money by flogging arms wherever the price is right, put on their Sunday cassocks and preach peace to the Middle East. From their lips the word sounds like a fart. On *Twenty-Four Hours* the other night, Kenneth Allsop interviewed a British arms merchant who has been selling to both Egypt and Israel. Admitting that he was having some doubts about his trade (he is now on the verge of an ill-earned retirement) he said that nevertheless the real question was: Am I my brother's keeper? and that the answer was No. The question was of course first put by Cain, whose flag flies high over most of the major cities of the world.

The more abstract war is made to seem, the more attractive it becomes. The advance of an army as represented by dynamic arrows swooping across the map can raise the same thrill as a child gets from playing draughts. Dubious score-sheets which say how many planes the government would have liked to have shot down only add to the game-like quality of news — you tot up the columns and kid yourself that someone is winning.

Wartime governments sometimes allow this process to be taken a step nearer reality by issuing photographs of one atrociously wounded soldier (our side) being lovingly nursed by his comrades, and another picture of dozens of prisoners (their side) being handed cups of water (see under Sir Philip Sidney, gallantry of). Such poses represent a caricature of war's effect on human beings.

What have the Arabs been doing? Killing Jews.

What have the Jews been doing? Killing Arabs.

Even that doesn't get us far in the direction of reality. To add statistics saying how many were killed takes us only an inch nearer.

Who is killed? What were they like? I would like to see every government in the world held accountable to the United Nations for every human being it kills, either in war or in peace. I don't just mean a statistic published in a secret report. I mean that all the newspapers of the country responsible should carry the name of the person killed, his photograph, address, number of his dependants and the reason why he was killed. (We often do as much for the victims of plane crashes.)

This would mean that in some countries the press would be swamped with death reports and even mammoth death supplements. (Well, what *about* the advertisers?) But I want more.

I would like every death inflicted by any government to be the subject of a book published at the state's expense. Each book would give an exhaustive biography of the corpse and would be illustrated by photographs from his family album if any, pictures he painted as a child and film stills of his last hours. In the back cover would be a long-playing disc of the victim talking to his friends, singing, talking to his wife and children and interviewed by the men who killed him.

The text would examine his life, his tastes and interests, faults and virtues, without trying to make him any more villainous or heroic than he was. It would be prepared by a team of writers appointed by the United Nations. The final chapter would record the explanations of the government which killed him and a detailed account of the manner of his death, the amount of bleeding, the extent of burns, the decibel count of screams, the amount of time it took to die and the names of the men who killed him.

One book for every killing. I realize that this would take some planning. Each soldier would have to be accompanied by an interviewing, camera and research team in order to record the details of any necessary victim.

Most factories would turn out printing presses, most graduates would automatically become biographers of the dead. Bombing could only take place after individual examination of every person to be bombed. The cost of killing would be raised to such a pitch that the smallest war would lead to bankruptcy and only the most merciful revolution could be afforded. Hit squarely in the exchequer — the only place where they feel emotion — chauvinist governments might be able to imagine, for the first time, the true magnitude of the obscenity which they mass-produce.

This is no bloody whimsy. I want a real reason for every killing.

GOSSIP COLUMN

Mrs Sinjohn Smackers down on the beauty farm on a diet of peasant juice and dungeon sweepings feels a small, star-shaped pain in her palatial stomach as she worries whether god is dead.

Horace Grindmate contemplates whether his mortgaged artistic talent can better be served by an advertising campaign for gold plated broad beans or by a magazine devoted to the pornography of rolls-royce engines.

Sir Thomas Margarine, as he invents Follicle Gas, which turns hair into snakes, considers an indiscretion with both his laboratory assistants.

Somewhere in South America, an old woman gives five onions to a quiet man with a knapsack who smells of two months in the mountains.

THE VIOLENT GOD (from *Move Over, Jehovah*)

Barbed wire all around the Garden of Eden
Adam was conscripted for the First World War
And it's still going on, and it's still going strong —
Hail to the violent god.

The old survivor said: I was in Belsen,
I'm grateful to God because he got me out of Belsen,
When I die please bury me in Belsen —
Hail to the violent god.

The god of hunger eats the people of India
The god of law and order spends most of his time
Smiling at the back of torture rooms —
Hail to the violent god.

Children were smitten with parents.
The black man was smitten with the white man.
The white man was smitten with the motor car —
Hail to the violent god.

Spastics teach us how to have pity
Leukaemia teaches us the dangers of anarchy
Schizophrenia teaches us sanity —
Hail to the violent god.

OLD TESTAMENT NEW TESTAMENT
or
HIS EYE IS ON THE BLONDE IN THE THIRD ROW

Tugging at his zippers,
Sweat in waterfalls down his leathers,
God used to scream into the mike.
Blood-lightning spurted from the speakers
And the sparks were in his hair — yeah.

Then he decided to try for the family audience.

SNAPS

drinks brandy all the time
at his age
he deserves it

small dog slowly
waves her tail
at the sun

bad morning
the ceiling of his skull
has measles

those berserk lambs
suddenly apply the brakes
wrong mother

THE GREAT BELL IN PAUL ROBESON'S CHEST

the great bell	speaks
the great bell	cast in blood
the great bell	speaks
the great bell	over the sea
the great bell	through the air
the great bell	across the land
the great bell	speaks
the great bell	freedom
the great bell	equality
the great bell	brotherhood
the great bell	speaks
the great bell	now
	now
	now
the great bell	speaks
the great bell	weeping
	thinking
	laughing
	dreaming
the great bell	loving
the great bell	speaks
the great bell	cast in blood
the great bell	speaks

THINKS: I'LL FINISH THESE VIETS BY BUILDING AN ELECTRONICALLY OPERATED PHYSICAL BARRIER RIGHT ALONG THEIR SEVENTEENTH PARALLEL!!!

(For John Arden and Margaretta D'Arcy)

1. Thousands of miles of invisible fencing
   Distinguishable only by the balding badness of the earth
   And a slight electric shimmer in the air.

   But if you throw raw hamburger towards the sky
   It comes down grilled.

2. The Marine shouted:
   'I don't mind fighting Charlie,
   But not with my back to a goddam
   Electronically operated physical barrier.'

3. We have stopped lifting our electronic barrier
   For one hour daily at Checkpoint Harold.
   We don't mind the refugee double-deckers heading north,
   But sod this constant rumbling southwards
   Of enormous invisible wooden horses.

4. If the barrier fails
   We are going to bring in volcanoes.

5. 'I just pissed against that
   Electronically operated physical barrier,'
   Boasted the police dog to his bitch,
   'And eighty-two square miles got devastated.'

6. Tom Sawyer drew a line in the dust with his toe:
   'Step over that and I'll burn your skin off.'

7. What we really need
   Is an electronically operated physical barrier
   Around the United States.

PEACE OF MIND

Through my lugubrious eyes,
Indoors, outdoors, at home, abroad,
In my head or out of it,
I keep seeing bad images
Superimposed on picture postcard views.
The people of Edinburgh
Sleepwalking through a cyclone of flame.
The plague-carts coming back to Cheapside.
The sounds of torture seeping
From a back room in a pub near Snowdon.

Failing to look on the bright side
Of cancer and Christianity,
I'm so jagged-headed and unsatisfied.

Surely I can erect a little tent of contentment.
It shall be orange-coloured
And I'll carry it all folded under
My private, tawny armpit.
And when I'm overwhelmed by the fumes of blood
In a lecture theatre or a sitting-room —
Into my contentment I'll creep.

But what can I be contented about?
Right. My height.
I'm not proud of my height, but I'm easy with it.
I don't have to duck under bridges
Or climb a chair to reach a doorhandle.
Nobody calls me lofty or shorty.
I've never been embarrassed by my height,
Not having visited Japan.

Five foot eleven inches —
Nothing special, but not bad going.
Five foot eleven inches.
My height. About right.

Five foot eleven inches . . .
All right, but my brother's six feet tall.

DEAR SIR

I have read your Manifesto with great interest but it says nothing about singing.

LOST LOVE POEM

One day they'll manufacture eggs,
The formula for snowflakes will be clear
And love explained — that's not the day
I think about, the day I marked on my calendar . . .

Because they appreciate their legs,
Simple creatures will career
Through boundless grass. One day, the day
I think about, the day I marked on my calendar . . .

In the classroom the boy with ragged fingernails
Flicks a note to the girl whose hair solidifies
All the light there is. The note says:
Some day, when I'm grown up, some day —
It falls between the floorboards . . .

HISTORICAL POEM

The first rocket to land on Mars
Was eaten

SLOGAN TIME

MEN ARE OUTNUMBERED BY TREES

THERE ARE EVEN MEAN-MOUTHED WOMEN CALLED MOLLY

HOPE IN A THOUSAND YEARS

THE PISTOL WITH WHICH HITLER SHOT HIMSELF WAS VERY BEAUTIFUL

LONGING IS TOO LONG

FIGHT MADNESS WITH JOKES

JOAN OF ARC IS IRRELEVANT

EGGS ARE APPROVED BY THE DESIGN CENTRE

EVERY TIME AN M.P. OPENS HIS MOUTH — ANTS WALK OUT

GLOBAL FOOD RATIONING OR ARMAGEDDON

DREAMS ARE TOO SMALL TO SHARE

GET READY FOR CONSCRIPTION — LEARN TO SHOOT

CLERGY ARE PLAINCLOTHES MEN IN FANCY DRESS

THE MARRIAGE OF HEAVEN AND HELL IS O.K., BUT WHAT ABOUT THE
CHILDREN?

A COUNTRY DIARY

As March melts into April, the jovial countryman breathes a sigh of relief which is visible from neighbouring farms. The winter's growth of ice, by now as thick as a blacksmith's thigh, has been carefully removed, a perfect disc, from the duckpond, and rolled without breakage to join the cylindrical pile of ice discs in the refrigerated silo. The last of the new-born lambs has been christened and tethered in his kennel of weather-chewed Yorkshire stone.

Spring bubbles in the jovial countryman's veins as he strides out, flame-thrower in hand, to rid the world of moles. On his wrist perches his faithful vulture, Tray.

The jovial countryman, face as red as a rabbit torn in half, spots Bob the Mole scurrying from scarecrow to scarecrow. Tray the Vulture registers a sharp intake of breath. Matt the Sheepdog flings aside his disguise. Cat the Cat raises a silhouetted claw against the bulbous scarlet of the seven p.m. sun. Crouch the Ferret clacks open and shut in the pocket of his master, the jovial countryman.

Bob the Mole flattens himself against a millstone. But it is not a millstone. Fergus the Tractor thunders down the flinty track, erupting through the coppice, regurgitating diesel in the form of rearward exhaust clouds, black clouds, death signals.

The serried animals jump upon Bob the Mole. Bob the Mole is dead. The feast over, all the animals return to their trenches. The jovial countryman plods down the lines, rewarding the good, punishing the bad.

A PARTY POLITICAL BROADCAST ON BEHALF OF THE BURIAL PARTY

SPOKESMAN:

Already our government has enforced the four freedoms:
Freedom to speak if you have nothing to say.
Freedom from fear if you stay in your shelter.
Freedom from want if you do what we want
And freedom from freedom.

But yesterday we, the British Government,
Detected, thanks to our spider's web of sundaypapers
And bloodshot radar traps,
Two mutineers scowling from your moderate ranks.

POLICE CONSTABLE BOOTHEAD:

At two in the morning I found the accused,
A man and a woman, both unclothed,
Sprawling across their mammoth bed.
(The mammoth is being held in custody at Disneyland.)
Their eyes were shut, and they grinned
Like a couple of pink grand pianos.
When asked why they were smiling with their eyes shut,
The accused informed me (in song):
'We are happy.'
I made a note of that at the time.

JUDGE:

What was that word again?

PROSECUTOR:

Happy, milord,
An expression common among delinquents.
It means — irresponsible.
Extensive chromosome and corpuscle counts,
Exhaustive spiritual testing
And a touch of the old Doctor Scholl revealed

That the male and female citizen were both addicted
To one of the most dangerous drugs on the list —
Exhibit A — Love —
Highly addictive, producing hallucinations,
For example:
Fats Waller fornicating downwards
At the wheel of a purple-striped cloud
To play The Resurrection of South America —
This love-drug can remove
The user's interest in moneyandproperty
And in killing in order to defend
Moneyandproperty.

JUDGE:

Stop it, I can't bear it.

SPOKESMAN:

The lovers were found guilty of not being guilty.
Their obscene craving was hard to cure
But a succession of secret licemen did their best.
They can hardly be blamed if the gasping lovers died
After ten days apart, ten days apart.
They died with their grins on, both of them drowned
In the same daydream,
The same degenerate lagoon.

Freedom to speak if you have nothing to say.
Freedom from fear if you stay in your shelter.
Freedom from want if you do what we want.
Freedom from freedom, freedom from sanity
And freedom, finally, from life.

IT IS LIKELY THAT DURING THE NEXT TEN YEARS
YOU WILL BE CALLED UPON TO DIE FOR FREEDOM.

FOUND POEM: AN ENGLISHMAN COMMENTS ON THE RETURN OF ROGER CASEMENT'S BODY TO IRELAND

That'll make room for one more nigger raging queer he was . . .

HOLDING MY WATER UNDER BREATH

Washed my skin and shaved my chin and washed my skin again.
My suit was suavely dark and darkly suave.
I joined a constellation
Of the washed white, the suavely shaven.

martini, martini, martini, martini, martini, martini.

My skull was a martini glass,
My brain the olive.
My face began to dirt over, to sprout stubble.
I werewolfed.
Happlily, I began to make trouble.

G.I. JOE

Have you heard the big news on TV?
Have you heard the big news on TV?
On the land
In the air
On the sea
Have you heard the big news on TV?

Halt, who goes there?
G.I. Joe! Who?
G.I. Joe, that's who!
G.I. Joe! G.I. Joe!

He's the password to a merry Christmas because he's the toy soldier
Santa Claus will put beneath your Christmas tree if you tell
your folks about him. They'll enjoy watching you play with your
G.I. Joe too!

Join the fun with G.I. Joe
G.I. Joe G.I. Joe
Fighting man from head to toe
G.I. Joe G.I. Joe

Halt, who goes there?

Everybody's hero is
G.I. Joe G.I. Joe
Everybody's dream come true
G.I. Joe G.I. Joe
Looks alive and acts alive
Almost eleven inches tall
21 movable parts
G.I. Joe G.I. Joe

Run
Walk
Climb
Crawl
Throw grenades

E

He's tremendous

G.I. Joe G.I. Joe
G.I. Joe G.I. Joe

Uniforms for every service
All he needs for every action
Rifles
Machine guns
Flame throwers
Sandbags
Tents
Communication gear
Scuba suits
G.I. Joe G.I. Joe

From coast to coast boys are joining the G.I. Joe Club and
becoming official collectors of G.I. Joes and equipment.

Have you heard the big news on TV?
Have you heard communications gear?
Have you been eleven inches tall?
Have you joined the sandbags on TV?
Fun grenade fun grenade
Fun flame fun gun
21 movable heads
Have you been eleven rifles tall?

Flame thrower from head to toe
G.I. Joe G.I. Joe
Join the flame with G.I. Joe
G.I. Joe G.I. Joe
From coast to coast
Boys are joining
Boys are running
Boys are climbing
Boys are crawling

From flame to flame
Santa's throwing
Rifle trees

Christmas guns
Christmas dreams
Christmas flames
scuba suits scuba suits scuba suits scuba suits
Join the fun join the fun
TV run
TV crawl
Dreams eleven inches tall
Flames eleven inches tall
On the land
In the air
On the sea
Flames eleven inches tall
Head to toe head to toe
Flame dreams flame dreams
Dream alive and flame alive
G.I. Joe G.I. Joe
G.I. Joe G.I. Joe
Everybody's dream come true . . .

Halt, who goes there?

EARLY SHIFT ON THE EVENING STANDARD NEWS DESK

Fog Chaos Grips South

A thick blanket of fog lay across Southern England this morning like a thick blanket —

'Don't let's call it a thick blanket today Joe, let's call it a sodden yellow eiderdown.'

'Are you insane?'

SEX MANIAC HIM GOOD
(from *The Second Mrs Tanqueray*)

We done it with pictures we done it with words
pounds and dollars and all
With hoare-belisha beacons and thunderbirds
at the money-fuckers' ball

Grabbed 'em by the scruff of the groin
pounds and dollars and all
Pumped 'em full of the slippery coin
at the money-fuckers' ball

Fifteen suicides screwing all night
pounds and dollars and all
Rolled in a ball down a mountain of shite
at the money-fuckers' ball

Money money money money come in a shower
pounds and dollars and all
Give me a stand like the Post Office Tower
at the money-fuckers' ball

Fucked the Bank of England and caught the pox
pounds and dollars and all
Jumped the Atlantic and buggered Fort Knox
at the money-fuckers' ball

One blind bankrupt couldn't get a screw
pounds and dollars and all
Tossed himself off with an I.O.U.
at the money-fuckers' ball

CALYPSO'S SONG TO ULYSSES
(from *Lash Me To The Mast!*)

My hands are tender feathers,
They can teach your body to soar.
My feet are two comedians
With jokes your flesh has never heard before.

So try to read the meaning
Of the blue veins under my skin
And feel my breasts like gentle wheels
Revolving from your thighs to your chin.

And listen to the rhythm
Of my heartbeat marking the pace
And see the visions sail across
The easy-riding waters of my face.

What is sweeter than the human body?
Two human bodies as they rise and fall.
What is sweeter than two loving bodies?
There is nothing sweeter at all.
Lose yourself, find yourself,
Lose yourself again
On the island of Calypso.

UNFULFILLED SUICIDE NOTE

because there is a golden plastic arrow on the desk in front of me
because my stomach is heavy and drags downwards
because I cannot find anything
because I cannot understand anything
because I am afraid of everyone
because there is a small amount of snow on the ground outside

MISERABLE SINNERS

Now I know that revolutionary Catholic priests have died fighting for freedom and socialism in South America, and Quaker schools are smashing, and Donald Soper's all right in his place, and some of the sayings of Jesus are worthy of William Blake — but to hell with organized religion.

In Ireland, the basic human needs of liberty, equality and fraternity go to blazes while the two big local superstitions fight it out.

If the professionals in the churches believe in Christ, why don't they work as he did? Jesus didn't take scholarships so he could study to become a rabbi. He didn't ask for a temple and a vicarage and a salary and a pension scheme. He didn't push for exclusive propaganda rights in schools.

To Jesus, the Churches of England and Rome would have been strictly science fiction. Vast, rich propaganda machines, thriving on spiritual blackmail.

He worked differently. He told as much of the truth as he could until they killed him — like many other good men, religious and irreligious. I've met many people like that, most of them members of no church, most of them completely unknown.

If the churches cared for this world, they would extract their hooks from their people, disestablish, disperse and house the people instead of God. De-escalate organized religion and some of the most hopeless political situations in the world would become clearer, even soluble. Even Ireland. Even the Middle East.

If you detect personal bitterness in the above, you are damn right. I will declare my interest. For a few years I attended a school where evangelism was the dominant religion. We used to go to camp in North Wales for intensive Bible readings and declarations of conversion.

The message sank in deep, and the message was guilt. And the punishment for guilt was Hell. I was taught the ugliness and vileness of the body. I was taught terror. The Hell we were threatened with was the Hell of the sermon in *Portrait of the Artist as a Young Man.*

In short, we were children with no defences, and we were violated by holy Hitchcocks. It took me about fifteen years to shake off most of that fear and disgust. I don't know what happened to the others.

Sure, this was an extreme case. Sure, it was way back in the nineteen-forties. But Frankenstein's monster (alias the Church of Christ) keeps rolling along, crushing children as it rolls.

QUESTION: But what would you put in the place of organized religion?

ANSWER: Omnicreed.

QUESTION: What is Omnicreed?

ANSWER: A custom-built religion, which incorporates the most imaginative ideas of all religions and rejects the boring, terror-laden and anti-imaginative concepts.

QUESTION: Can you give me some examples?

ANSWER: You bet your sweet soul. The Anti-Imagination, known and rejected among Omnicreed initiates as The Brown Lump, embraces such concepts as the Sabbath, clergymen, popery, no popery and Cliff Richard in Westminster Abbey. On the other hand, Omnicreed awards its Good Churchkeeping Certificate to such doctrines as The Immaculate Unction of Pope Joan, Nirvana as a Motel, the Bank of England Formation Dancing Team, Bulldozer Rallies, Calvin as the Inventor of Milk Chocolate, Nationalized Delicatessens, Zen Washing Lines and the Company of Dogs.

QUESTION: Have you got a light?

THE EGGS O' GOD

Last Thursday God manifested himself as a barrage balloon with varicose veins and descended on the Vatican. I'm shrivelling, he shouted to the Pope, once I was bigger than the Universe but now I'm shrinking fast. The bulk of God lolled in St Peter's Square, deflating soon to the size of a double-decker bus. Quick, cried God, before I vanish, one last request. When I've disappeared, put my eggs in a jar, keep in a cool place and run a world-wide search for a warm-hearted virgin. Let her hatch the eggs and then you'll find —

But by now God is a hissing football, and now he is a grapefruit, now a grape, and now the grape has exploded and nothing is left in the Square but the Eggs of God.

Four Switzers armed with money-trowels shovelled the golden spawn into a lucent white container and bore it to the Papal fridge.

At two in the morning a whisky cardinal staggered in, his stomach growling for a snack. Unfortunately he fancied caviar . . .

The Pope has risen frae his bed
On his twa holy legs
And doon the marble staircase gaed
Tae see the sacred eggs

O wha has stolen the Eggs o' God
Gae seek him near and far
O wha has stolen the Eggs o' God
Frae the Gentleman's Relish jar

Then up and spak the Cardinal
His voice was like a Boeing
O I hae eaten the Eggs o' God
And I'm eight miles tall, and growing . . .

FUNNYHOUSE OF A NEGRO

(for Adrienne Kennedy)

A head
beating against a wall
A beautiful head
beating against a wall
The beautiful head of a woman
beating against a wall
The beautiful head of a woman with her wrists and ankles chained
beating against a wall

A million beautiful heads
beating against a wall

And the first brick is shaken loose
topples
and begins to fall

IN OTHER WORDS, HOLD MY HEAD

'Capitalism — ', I started, but the barman hopped out of a pipkin.
'Capitalism', he countered, 'that's a flat and frothless word.
I'm a good labourman, but if I mentioned capitalism
My clientele would chew off their own ears
And spit them down the barmaid's publicized cleavage.'
'All right,' I obliged, 'don't call it capitalism,
Let's call it Mattiboko the Mighty.'

'Exploitation —', I typed, but the Editor appeared unto me,
A spike in one hand, a fiery pound note in the other.
'I'm a good liberal, but you're going out on a lamb —
You don't catch Burnem Levin writing about exploitation —
A million readers would gouge their eyes out,
Think of that, like two million pickled onions in the cornflakes.'
'Hold the back page,' I surlied, 'sod exploitation,
I'll retitle it The Massimataxis Incorporated Supplement.'

'Oppression and mass-murder —', I opined straight into the
                                                   camera.
'Cut!' yelled the director, cutting off his head with a
                                            clapperboard.
'I'm a good fascist, but if you use that language
Half your viewers are going to
Tear the lids off their TV sets,
Climb inside, pour Horlicks over their heads
And die of calculated combustion.
Too late now to balance the programme
With a heartsofoak panel of our special experts
Who are all oppressors and mass-murderers.'
'You know the market,' I wizened,
'Oppression and mass-murder are out this year —
I'll christen them Gumbo Jumbo the Homely Obblestrog Specta-
                                                   cular.'

This was my fearless statement:
The Horror World can only be changed by the destruction of
Mattiboko the Mighty,

The Massimataxis Incorporated Supplement
And Gumbo Jumbo the Homely Obblestrog Spectacular.

Audience reaction was quite encouraging.

A LEAFLET TO BE DROPPED ON CHINA

(This is a translation back into English of a dialogue between two ordinary Britons. This dialogue is to be printed as the first in a series of leaflets to be dropped on China in order to explain about Western Civilization.)

BILL.   I say, Fred, what do you think about Her Majesty The Queen?

FRED.   Well, Bill, I am bound to say that I do not envy Her Her job!

BILL.   What? But surely Her life must be both enjoyable and rewarding. With those dogs and pearls and soldiers and things.

FRED.   Would you say so, Bill? But Her Majesty has many onerous duties to perform. Is not Her motto, I Serve?

BILL.   No Fred, I think it is God Save the Queen. I saw a film starring Her on television. She was waving to a group of policemen who were guarding a patch of snow.

FRED.   Be that as it may, Bill. She is expected to lend Her name to charities of every sort, to attend with the horse racing and to shake hands among other things with members of the Family of Commonwealth without regard for race, colour, creed or money.

BILL.   Well, Fred, when you put it like that old comrade, I suppose Her average day must be a full and demanding one! But surely She is well paid for Her efforts!

FRED.   Aha Bill, you have fallen into a common fallacy. Her Majesty the Queen is by no means well paid considering! The income from Her own estates provides the wherewithal for Her everyday expenses like ice creams, er and pearls! !

BILL.   Well, well, that is surprising!

FRED.   And on top of that to boot, She is also Chief of the Church of England! ! !

BILL.   Good heavens, Fred! I would not like to work as hard! I would not like to be the Queen for all the tea in China!!

FRED.   No more, Bill, would I! ! ! !

68

ROYAL POEMS

The *Daily Telegraph* wrote asking me: 'Could you, for instance, let us have some verse on how you see the relationship that exists between the Prince of Wales and the Welsh people? Obviously it is quite impossible for us to let you have a clear brief, but what we hope to achieve is something that will in some way reflect the Welsh mood as we see it, or even as they see it.' I responded by return of post with the following:

TO CHARLES WINDSOR-MOUNTBATTEN

Royalty is a neurosis.
Get well soon.

The *Daily Telegraph* rejected my contribution politely, but they'd started something and, after a week's research in which I established beyond reasonable doubt my claim to the throne of England, I wrote a series of regal bits in my new persona as the Rightful King of England.

LOYAL ODE TO MYSELF ON MY INSTALLATION AS PRINCE OF YORKSHIRE

Applauded by the loyal West Riding drizzle
I progressed up the A65
Bearing the symbol of my temporal power,
An iced lolly, very cold and powerfully purple.
Under my purple breath
I swore eternal fealty to myself
Against all manner of folks.
Nobody threw any eggs at ME.

DECREE TO ALL MEMBERS OF THE CHURCH OF ENGLAND

We, His Majesty, the Rightful King of England,
Do hereby publish and decree
And do most hideously command on pain of pain
That all baptized members of our Church of England
Shall sell all that they have
And bring the wherewithal therefrom

To our most Royal Treasury.
We shall await your loyal tributes
At the summit of Primrose Hill
At noon on October 24th this year,
Cash please, no cheques.
Yours sincerely,
Defender of the Faith.

THE ROYAL PREROGATIVE OF MERCY

Put that woman down at once!
We know she's upset you,
We know she's got a face
Like a breach of the peace,
But give her back her horse,
Return her knickers.
We are a merciful King
Even to women in military uniform
Who pretend to be the Queen of England.

MOSES ON SENSUALITY
(from *Move Over, Jehovah*)

Aaron, I've had a few thoughts and I want you to pass them on.
The main thought is that everyone shares the same basic need.
Watch a baby. It likes to be cuddled. It has to be cuddled or it
would become distorted. This has been proved with monkeys.
Animal contact.

Now watch two lovers in their teens. They like touching each
other. They can hardly bear not to touch each other. They like
making love, which is a combination of skin friction and rhythmic
stimulus. Animal contact.

Now watch an old lady. She's so old that nobody will live with
her except cats. So she moves from one cat to another, touching
them as she walks, as if she would fall over if she wasn't touching
a cat. Animal contact.

Right, Aaron. Everyone longs for animal contact. Now think of
these Children in our charge. Every time they touch each other —
a hand brushing a knee under the table at lunchtime, a shoulder
against a back in the queue for manna, every time they touch,
there is an exchange of energy between their bodies.

And that energy can build and build until it becomes a human
hurricane. And at the eye of the cyclone — what's there?

Sin, Aaron. The mantrap under the turf of the Garden of Eden.
The huge mouth in the ground. And the mouth has teeth, Aaron,
teeth which tear and grind the soul.

Sin with its body clothed in slime. Sin, its nostrils filled with the
guilty stinks of lavatories and beds. Sin which smiles, sin which
kills.

And so, when I feel the need to touch someone, I go into battle.
I grip the arms of my chair more tightly. I clamp my jaws together like a carpenter's vice. I may shake. My face may bulge
with red veins. I may stutter. But I fight my battle. And, with
the help of God, I am victorious.

F

FOR A MEDICAL DICTIONARY

Egghead

Your head becomes a soft-boiled egg.
Your hands' protective cradle rocks your forehead
And far inside, the restless baby,
The yolk,
Stirs.

Atmospheric Exdigestion

The patient is attacked from outside
By clusters of powerful farts
Attempting to get into him.

Festival

On Monday, with ceremonial ceremony
And a fanfare of funfairs,
We inaugurated
Be Kind To The Clitoris Week.
We finally found it
At 5.30 p.m. on Friday.

MUSICAL

Musical rain clouds begin to play
Musical lunatics sway round the corner
Musical girls slide down the hay
Music visits the charcoal-burner

ODE TO ENOCH POWELL

The vulture is an honest man
He offers no apology
But snaps the fingers from the hand
And chews them with sincerity

Birmingham Council are bidding for the Berlin Wall.
There's swastikas sprouting in the ground round Bradford Town
Hall.
Edward Heath and Harold Wilson are dancing cheek to cheek —
Everybody getting ready for Kindness to Vultures Week.

The vulture is a gentleman
He does not stoop to kill
But watches murders from a height
Then drops to eat his fill

The Press is so excited that the Press can hardly speak.
There's red stuff dripping from the corner of Nabarro's beak.
You can say that white is right, but it looks like black is bleak —
Everybody getting ready for Kindness to Vultures Week.

The vulture is a Christian man
He goes to church on Sunday,
Prays to God to give him strength
To tear a corpse on Monday

The Widow of Wolverhampton's been elected Queen
And her letter-box is fitted with an automatic flushing machine.*
She's translating the speeches of Hitler into Ancient Greek —
Everybody getting ready for Kindness to Vultures Week.

*Historical footnote: Powell told England how a lonely landlady
in Wolverhampton was persecuted by immigrants, who pushed
alien turds through her letter-box. After this speech, Powell received 100,000 letters, most of them supporting him. So the
widow wasn't the only one to get shit through the letter-box.

INVOLVEMENT

QUESTION (from the *London Magazine*):

In most European countries, and in America, writers are becoming involved, one way or another, in public manifestations of protest. As an English writer, do you feel that working on your own terms is more important than taking a practical part in organizing public opinion?

In other words, in the continuing debates — about race, class, violence, war, financial priorities — that crucially affect our lives, are you for the writer in any way as polemicist, or do you believe that his instinct as an artist is ultimately the real test of his integrity?

ANSWER:

SCENE: an alley.

(A MAN is being beaten up by TWO SECRET POLICEMEN. An ENGLISH WRITER approaches.)

> MAN
> Help!

> ENGLISH WRITER
> Well, that may be what you think you want. But I've got to work on my own terms.

> MAN
> Help!

(TWO SECRET POLICEMEN put the boot in.)

> ENGLISH WRITER
> Look, I don't like this any more than you do. But I've got to follow my own instinct as an artist.

MAN (spitting teeth)
Yes, well that's ultimately the real
test of your integrity.

(The beating up continues.
ENGLISH WRITER pisses off to write a poem about ants.)

CURTAIN

DREAM CHANT (from *The Body*)

Dream about

electric wallpaper
hovercraft boots
blue suede robots and vertical take-off underwear

Dream about

dolphin steaks
nuclear umbrellas, bacteriological cigars
and package tours of the dark side of the Earth

Dream about

disposable children
jumbo-jet prostitutes
and Mantovani piped to the foetus in the womb

oh, vote for technology, my honey-pissing darling,
vote for Me.

WE CALL THEM SUBNORMAL CHILDREN
(from *The Body*)

They are here, they are here,
they are very far away.

Perhaps they see exciting visions
in the hollows of their hands.
Perhaps they can hear music we are deaf to

but I think their hearts trudge
and that their days trudge

for the way they sort of stand
the way they sort of speak

laboriously expresses one word only
wounded   wounded   wounded

We are taking a deep breath before the long slow dive through
space to Mars.

We have not yet explored these island people.

They are here.
They will not go away.

FINAL CHANT (from *The Body*)

Long live the child
Long live the mother and father
Long live man

Long live this wounded planet
Long live the good milk of the air
Long live the spawning rivers and the mothering oceans
Long live the juice of the grass
and all the determined greenery of the globe
Long live the surviving animals
Long live the earth, deeper than all our thinking

We have done enough killing

Long live the man
Long live the woman
Who use both courage and compassion
Long live their children

LET ME TELL YOU THE THIRD WORLD WAR IS GOING TO SEPARATE THE MEN FROM THE BOYS

SON. Make sure the black blind fits the window,
Don't let the light fly out.
Where is the war tonight?

FATHER. No, this is peacetime.
You are safely tucked up in England.
Sleep tight, happy dreams.

SON. Listen, Daddy, are they ours or theirs?

FATHER. They are owls, they are nobody's
Responsibility. This is peace.

SON. Today I lost a battle.
I feel like mud.

FATHER. Snuggle down, snuggle down,
Tomorrow you will win two battles.

SON. Yes, and I will feel like mud.

FATHER. Grow up, this is self-pitying hyper-bollocks.
Nobody is really, actually trying to
Literally kill us.

SON. Yes they are, Daddy,
Yes they are.

WE CAN'T DO ANYTHING ALL THE TIME

But we should be able to look at the ocean
and say

O

and let our

O

balloon away to pop on the point
of a far wave.

But every time we choose a word
we choose sides.

All right, we have to
analyze, explain, work out the cost,
yes but not all the time.

All right, we have to
surrender to slumber and
the wonders of the world,
yes but not all the time.

Struggle, defend, attack — sure —
but while our eyes fire at the enemy
may our hands, grooving the putty
round multi-coloured windows
or balancing the brick, which has no owner,
into its place, continue to create

a city in which the newborn will unroll
laughing to be born into such a city

and old men will cry their sorrow

O

when it is time to leave

THE UNIVERSE IS AN OUTSIZE MICROCOSM

As I was plodding to the parsonage
I met a giant vivid orange ostrich.
He said its name was Gaston MacWhoreson,
But she laid an egg as big as a person
Thus proving my gene group's motto which is:
There are no bigger liars than ostriches.

SOLID CITIZENS

Let us praise the dead

Snug in their wooden homes
Under the aerials of Christ
Keeping themselves to themselves.

They do not strike or demonstrate;

Should they do so
They would lose the support
Of a sympathetic public.

21st CENTURY WEREWOLF (from *The Hotpot Saga*)

I was zooming round the universe feeling like Desperate Dan
I was bombing them at random in the hope of hitting Charlie Chan
I looked and saw a continent without a single man
Which they told me was Asia but it looked more like Aberfan

Ride the nightmare
Jump upon its hairy back
Ride the nightmare
Ride until your mind goes black
It's the 21st Century Werewolf
And it's coming this way

Well the charity lady wiped the diamonds from her eyes and said
I've been saving all my pennies but the African dead stay dead
I'm sending them Elastoplast and Dunlopillo bread
But they wrote me a letter saying, Send us guns instead

Ride the nightmare
Jump upon its hairy back
Ride the nightmare
Ride until your mind goes black
It's the 21st Century Werewolf
And it's coming this way.

Well the rich white Englishman can easily ignore the rest
For the poor are just a bore and who can use the starving and
                                        oppressed?
They're burning while you tell yourself there's nothing you can do
When their turn comes they'll do just the same for you

So ride the nightmare
Jump upon its hairy back
Ride the nightmare
Ride until your mind goes black
It's the 21st Century Werewolf
And it's coming this way.

HELLO ADRIAN

(for Adrian Henri)

Hello Adrian — I just crawled out the far side of Xmas to scrawl
          my report on the wall,
We breathed nothing but wine all the time till the group got liqui-
          dated on the twelfth day with turkey soup.
Well it was a feast of the beast and half the animals were kissing
          when they weren't pissing,
Though there were days when the haze turned jagged and I walked
          into a room full of stainless smiles and white tiles —

        But I will confess
I never had it
        Halfway up a pylon
Never had it
        Under the stage during a performance of Ibsen's
          An Enemy of the People
Never had it
        In the Whispering Gallery at St Paul's
Never had it
        Up against a parking meter

But where — it doesn't matter
When — it doesn't count
All you got to total
Is the total amount

        They're doing it for peace
        Doing it for war
        There's only one good reason
        For doing it for

(CHORUS) Fuck for fun (Fuck fuck, fuck for fun)
         Fuck for fun (Fuck fuck, fuck for fun)
         Fuck for fun (Fuck fuck, fuck for fun)
         Everybody want to (boom boom)
         Fuck for fun.

They're doing it in Paris
'Cos it tastes so sweet
They do it by the Mersey
'Cos they like that beat

They're doing it for Mother
Doing it for Freud
Reginald Plantagenet
Somerset-Boyd

(CHORUS)

They do it for publicity
Doing it for cash
Might as well be robots
The way they bash

They do it in Chicago
Just to fool the fuzz
They do it down in London
Just 'cos Mick Jagger does

(CHORUS)

They do it up in Edinburgh
With cannon balls
Newcastle girls do it
High on the walls

Now there's too little action
Too much talk
When the bottle's open
Throw away the cork

(CHORUS)

Well North Riding girls taste of cedarwood
South Riding girls cook the wildest pud
East Riding girls melt your soul like lard
West Riding girls well they try bloody hard
North East West South side by side
What you care so long as they ride

So ride your lover
Get on your little lover and ride

They do it in the Palace
To preserve the line
But we're going to do it
'Cos it feels so fine

I've got a red-hearted woman
I'm a socialist man
We've got a great leap forward
And a five year plan

(CHORUS)

An eye for an eye
Tit for tat
Batman fuck Robin
And Robin fuck a bat

Fuck for fun (Fuck fuck, fuck for fun)
Fuck for fun (Fuck fuck, fuck for fun)
Doesn't matter if you're incredibly old or absurdly
young

C'mon everybody and (boom boom)
Fuck for fun.

The following verses were written before Lyndon Johnson, at that time the most hated man on earth, was psychically assassinated by all that hatred.

ODE ON THE ASSASSINATION OF PRESIDENT JOHNSON

On the thousandth floor of the Texas Corpse Depository
A million dead people kneel at the windows,
Their terror-eaten eyes,
Their maggot-smitten eyes,
Their eyes — blistered, sliced, exploded —
Focusing down on the golden vehicle.
They wait, they have been waiting for many years.

And now, as the Presidential procession approaches,
The route is lined by waving copies of *Time* magazine
And cheering TV sets.
In offices along the way
Tickertape machines have been tearing office workers
Into hero-size confetti —
Folks, it's literally snowing flesh . . .

From the thousandth floor of the Texas Corpse Depository
A million bullets of blood converge.
There is a highway through the Presidential throat
And yellow metal, chilly but molten,
Pours from his jugular.

There is no need to panic.
Another President Johnson is being sworn in.
There is no need to panic.
A million dead people have been arrested,
Found guilty and killed again.
There is no need to panic,
There is an almost unlimited supply of President Johnsons.

So alter the score in the war between the rich and the poor.
Add one more unit to the Casualty Statistics Computer.
One eye for one million eyes —
He had it coming.

FROM THE STATEMENT OF A VIETNAMESE
BUDDHIST MONK

The secret police came to me in the middle of the night
and said: 'Do you believe in God?'

BYRON IS ONE OF THE DANCERS

His poems — they were glad with jokes, trumpets, arguments and
                                         flying crockery
                 Rejoice
He shook hearts with his lust and nonsense, he was independent as
                                         the weather
                 Rejoice
Alive, alive, fully as alive as us, he used his life and let life use him
                 Rejoice
He loved freedom, he loved Greece, and yes of course, he died for
                               the freedom of Greece
                 Rejoice

          And yes, this is a dance,
          and yes, beyond the glum farrago
          of TV cops after TV crooks
          in the blockheaded prison of TV —

          I hear the naked feet of Byron
          which skated once, powered by fascination
          over the cheerful skin of women's legs,
          I hear those two bare feet —
          One delicate and one shaped horribly —
          slap and thud, slap, thud, slap, thud,
          across the cracked-up earth of Greece,
          and yes, I hear the music which drives those feet
          and feel the arm of Byron round my shoulder
          or maybe it is round your shoulder
          Oh I feel your arm around my shoulder
          and yes, I know the line of dancers
          across the cracked-up earth of Greece
          stretches from sea to sea
          as the shrivelled mountains erupt into music
          and Byron and all the million dancers
          yes brothers and sisters, lovers and lovers,
          some lucky in life and delicately-skinned,
          some shaped horribly by want or torture,
          dance out the dance which must be danced

for the freedom of Greece
for the freedom of Greece

Dance
Rejoice
Dance
Rejoice

PAUSE

I was just about to say to my daughter:
Look what beautiful eyes that horse has.
When I suddenly stopped and thought:
Maybe horses aren't supposed to have eyes like that.

MY PARENTS

My father died the other day and I would like to write about him. Because I think of them together, this means also writing about my mother, who died several years ago.

About a thousand people called her Kay, most of them people she helped at some time, for she was what chintzy villains call a 'do-gooder'. Nobody ever called her that to her face or in my family's hearing; if they had, she'd have felt sorry for them. Both her brothers were killed in the First World War. She divided her life between loving her family, bullying or laughing innumerable committees into action rather than talk, giving, plotting happiness for other people, and keeping up an exuberant correspondence with several hundred friends.

She was not afraid of anyone. She was right. A Fabian near-pacifist, she encouraged me to argue, assuming right-wing positions sometimes so that I was forced to fight and win the discussion.

She tried to hoist the whole world on her shoulders. After each of her first two cancer operations, on her breasts, she seemed to clench her fists and double the energy with which she gave. She wasn't interested in unshared pleasure.

After the second operation she answered the door one day to a poor woman whom she didn't know. The woman asked where 'the wise woman' lived. My mother knew who she meant — a rich clairvoyant who lived down the road. Not trusting that particular witch, my mother asked what was wrong. The poor woman's doctor had told her that she must have a breast removed, and she was very scared. My mother said, but there's nothing to that, look — and she took out the two rolled socks which she kept in her empty brassière and threw them up into the sunlight and then caught them again. So the poor woman came in, drank tea, talked, forgot many fears, and went away knowing that she had seen the wise woman.

People called my father Jock. Face tanned from working in his garden, he survived the trenches of the First World War. He spoke very little. When he talked it was either very funny or very important. He only spoke to me about his war twice, and then briefly. In my teens I wrote a short, Owen-influenced poem about that war. My father read it, then told me of a friend who, during the lull between bombardments, fell to all fours and howled like an animal and was never cured.

Usually he avoided company. There was something in other people which frightened him. He was right. At the seaside he would sit on the farthest-out rock and fish peacefully. When visitors called at our house he would generally disappear into his jungle of raspberry canes and lurk.

Maybe there were twenty or thirty people in the world whose company he really enjoyed. They were lucky; he was a lovely man. Like Edward Lear, he was most at his ease with children, who instantly read, in the lines radiating from the corners of his eyes, that this was a man who understood their games and jokes.

After my mother's death, he was a desolated man. But when he remarried, very happily, light came back into his face and he learned to smile again. He was short and lean and had fantastic sprouting Scottish eyebrows. He was a research chemist, but that didn't mean he only took an interest and pride in my elder brother's scientific work. He let me see how glad he was that I wrote, and I still remember the stories he used to write for me and my brother.

A year or so before he died he was in London for the day. My father sometimes voted Tory, sometimes Liberal, but when he began to talk about Vietnam that day, his face became first red and then white with anger about the cruelty and stupidity of the war. I seldom saw him angry and never so angry as at that moment, a man of seventy, not much interested in politics, all the grief of 1914–18 marching back into his mind.

People sometimes talk as if the ideological conflicts between generations have to be fought out bloodily, as if it is inevitable that children should grow to hate their parents. I don't believe this. Our family was lucky: my brother and I were always free to choose for ourselves — knowing that, however odd our decisions, we were trusted and loved. We all loved one another and this love was never shadowed.

LOOSE LEAF POEM

(This is a diary of good and bad things, mostly for friends and
allies but with a few sections for enemies as well. It was written
in a peaceful room with a view of the Yorkshire Dales. In reading
it aloud, I often change the order of sections, talk in between
sections and leave out any part which doesn't seem relevant at
the time.)

There was a child danced with a child
The music stopped

* * * * * * * * * * * *

I stopped reading *The Wretched of the Earth*
Because you cannot read it all the time.

My stomach felt like outer space.
The sunday papers all sounded
Like bidders in a slave market.

I ate rapidly, alone,
Because I couldn't sit and eat with anyone,
Or look at anyone.

I glanced into the television's eye.
It was both bright and blind.

I was full of useless tears.
I did not use them.

* * * * * * * * * * * *

Who was the hooligan who ripped off all your skin, madam?

The North Atlantic Treaty Organization.

* * * * * * * * * * * *

Below my window, a stone wall begins,
swerves past a tree, drags its weight
upwards, almost collides with a second tree,

H

breaks for a gate, resumes,
and skitters over the horizon.
I watch the way it rides,
blonde stone in the blonde light of Yorkshire.

* * * * * * * * * * * *

Are you bored by pictures of burning people?
You will be bored to death.

They did the dying.
You did nothing.

Not a gesture, not a word, not a breath,
Not a flicker of one line of your face.

You said: There is nothing I can do.
As you said it you seemed so proud.

* * * * * * * * * * * *

There was a wretched danced with a wretched
The music began to burn.

* * * * * * * * * * * *

In the chapel-cold porridge of fear
Crouched the spirit of Edward Lear
　　　　Through the hole in his head
　　　　His agony bled
　　　　Till he changed to a Whale
　　　　And spouted a hail —
Cholomondley Champagne and the best Babylonian Beer.

* * * * * * * * * * * *

To　Ian Hamilton and A. Alvarez, Poetry Reviewers —
　　Get your blue hands
　　off the hot skin of poetry.

* * * * * * * * * * * *

96

My brain socialist
My heart anarchist
My eyes pacifist
My blood revolutionary

* * * * * * * * * * * *

The man who believes in giraffes would swallow anything.
There's been nothing about ostriches in the papers for months,
    somebody's either building an ostrich monopoly or
    herding them into concentration camps.
Butterflies fly zigzag because they want to fly zigzag.
I have looked into a hedgehog's face and seen nothing but goodness.
A huge ram stamps his foot — a million sheep charge and occupy
    the Bradford Wool Exchange.

* * * * * * * * * * * *

pip
pop
pip
pop
pip pip pip
pop

i am either a sound poet
or a bowl of Rice Crispies

* * * * * * * * * * * *

(to a friend who killed himself)

All that pain
double-bulging under your forehead
I wish you could have taken
a handful of today's Yorkshire snow
and pressed it to that pain.
You rummaged for peace
in the green country, in the eye of the sun,
in visions of Tibet,
brain-shaking drugs, black magic,

police stations, among the stones,
beneath the stones.
But the stones, which seemed so calm,
screamed into life in your hurt hands.
Simpler than you
I simply wish you were alive
walking among this snowfall.
I'm glad that all your pain is dead.

****

(to dogmatic men and automatic dogs)

I'm an entrist, centrist, Pabloite workerist
— Sweet Fourth International and never been kissed,
I've got a mass red base that's why I'd rather sit on the floor,
If you want to be a vanguard, better join Securicor.

My daddy was opportunistic
My mama was mystified
I want to be a movement
But there's no one on my side . . .

****

Never look out
You might see something bigger than you
Never go out
You might get your iambics dirty

Wine is a river
Flowing down to sleep
So climb in the boat
With your legitimate wife
No sharks   No storms
No underwater explosions

Never look out
The sun might punch you in the eye —

Stay home.

* * * * * * * * * * * *

I pulled on my solid granite gargoyle suit, borrowed a hunch from Sherlock Holmes and swung down from the turrets of Notre Dame just in time to rescue the naked Andromeda who was chained to King Kong in the middle of Red Square, Milwaukee.

Mark Antony immediately denounced me to a mob of Transylvanian peasants, who hurried me to the nearest oasis for a good guillotining.

Luckily for me the Flying Nun was power-diving down for a suicide raid on Moby Dick.

She noticed my plight, shot out a tentacle and scooped me into an echo chamber full of Dusty Springfields, thus foiling the machinations of Edgar Allen Fu Manchu, the Jackdaw of Zenda.

So you will understand why I am delighted to be here tonight to introduce a fourth member of fiction's Trolleybus Trinity — ladies and gentlemen, let's hear it for Miss Marlene Brontë.

* * * * * * * * * * * *

At the end of each adventure
Mighty Mouse stands, arms folded, on a pedestal,
Cheered by a crowd of infant mice.

Every Sunday
God is praised
In several million churches.

Mighty Mouse saved us from the Monster Cat!!!!

* * * * * * * * * * * *

In case the atmosphere catches on fire
The first thing to do will be to burn

* * * * * * * * * * * *

Your breath is like deodorant, your blood like Irish lager,
Your idea of paradise an infinite *Forsyte Saga*,
Your head belongs to Nato and your heart to the Playboy Club,
You're the square root of minus zero, playing rub-a-dub-dub
                                    in a Fleet Street pub.

Sit tight in your tower of money . . .

You've got a problem of identity, ooh what an intellectual shame,
You've got a million pseudonyms and can't recall your maiden
                                                    name,
You cannot tell your face from your arse or your supper from
                                                    your sex,
But you always remember who you are when it comes to
                                        signing cheques —

Sit tight in your tower of money . . .

                    * * * * * * * * * * * *

In case England catches on fire
The first thing to do will be to form a committee
To organize a week-end seminar
On Little-Known Conflagrations in Italian History
Or The Rise and Fall of the Safety Match in Literature and Life.

                    * * * * * * * * * * * *

Many thin men
saying: No.

But of course we've got to inside-out ourselves
and splash around in our own juice,
and the juice can't shine if you don't throw it up into the light,
and of course you're hard to hit if you keep dancing
and harder to hit if you make up your own dance as you dance,
and of course Tarzan is more exciting than Cecil Day Larkin
because he can MOVE, swinging through jungles of clubfooted
                                                    prose,

into your eye and out your navel,
and of course there's no perfect music,
no perfect words,

100

only the ridiculous beauty of man and woman
silly with each other,
pulling off their skins and swinging them round their heads,
becoming incredible fountains upon legs —

Many thin men
saying: No.

* * * * * * * * * * * *

There's a factory for making factories,
A sinking pool for learning to drown,
A university like a pencil sharpener
To whittle you down to a pinpoint.
There's a mean old weather machine
Churning out crapstorms
And a generation gap between
Me and what I used to be.
But the cities of horror,
Skull pavements, murder girders —
They're going to crumble away in our hands.

* * * * * * * * * * * *

The ice-cubes in my bloodstream decided to melt today.
I'd buy a moustache like everyone else
But I'm too attached to golden syrup.
There are hailstones big as hailstones, but I'm sure
They're not aimed at me.
Yes, Timbuctoo. I suddenly want to go to Timbuctoo.

* * * * * * * * * * * *

Grass pours down the hillside.
The stone wall gradually turns green.
A dead tree can keep its balance for years.

* * * * * * * * * * * *

You can't win.
Mary Queen of Scots invented high heel shoes to make her-
self look taller they cut her bloody head off. (John Walton.)

* * * * * * * * * * * *   **101**

Suddenly it hits me that it's May Day and I hadn't even noticed it
was April,
And was gazing over the floodlit fields at a group of socially-
minded cows,
And laughing to myself about the time Allen Ginsberg bared his
arse to the people in a whizzing-by train,
And marking passages in a book of Fidel Castro's speeches —
Quote — And then you hear a revolutionary say: They crushed us,
They organized 200 radio programmes, so many newspapers,
so many magazines, so many TV shows,
so many of this and so many of that — and one wants to ask him,
What did you expect?
That they would put TV, radio, the magazines, the newspapers,
the printing shops —
All this at your disposal?
Or are you unaware that these are the instruments of the ruling
class
Designed explicitly for crushing the Revolution? — unquote.
And I was also thinking of the pirhana fish grinning in the depths
of my bank manager's soul,
And I was looking through the B.B.C. Folk Club magazine and
trying to imagine the B.B.C. Folk,
And I was looking forward to a bit of bed with Celia in the
afternoon,
And my eyes kept returning to a letter from the poet Tim Daly,
Liquid blue handwriting between strict blue lines,
His words saying — quote —
As a whole, the support I have received has amazed me,
I had anticipated only antagonism.
Love be praised, I was wrong — unquote —
And I look again at his address:
Her Majesty's Prison, County Road, Maidstone, Kent.
Tim, aged twenty-one, who took his petrol bombs
To the Imperial War Museum
Because the Museum was teaching children war . . .
And so when it suddenly hits me that it's been May Day all day
And I should be feeling solidarity,
I think yes so I should, and yes I do, and so yes I write this down
As a demonstration of solidarity —

102

With the cows, who have now moved on,
With Allen Ginsberg, who has now moved on,
With Fidel Castro as he moves socialism onwards,
With Celia who moves me as we move together,
And with Tim Daly the poet,
Locked away for four years
So that England may be safe for the dead.

TO TIM DALY ON HIS 21st BIRTHDAY IN PRISON

I'm not allowed to send you a tree.

Shut your eyes now,
Try to receive what I'm trying to transmit to you —

A scarlet-breasted waterbird
        High
Above a forest scattered with
        Lakes

Family elephants in the Roman baths at Bath
Roller-skating over comic-strip tiles

Duke Ellington's sky
Going dark growing bright
Purple-shadow clouds at their love-play

A cake iced all over with a map of the world.
Colours of the countries flowing into each other

      Air
As kind as honey

      Funny wine
To make your skin laugh

Gentle faces gentle hands
Gentle voices singing love to you

And, visible and audible only to you,
A multi-coloured, madcap, musical
Birthday harem.

GUNS

They seem to have all the guns.
Most of the guns in Britain are
British/American government property
Police property
Or the property of gentry-gangsters
Who are British/American government property.

Nobody I love has a gun. Not in Britain.

The rich are rich because they fuck people about.
They call it the Quality of Leadership
And they have special school-machines producing
Leaders to fuck people about.

People with guns
Tend to fuck other people about.
The people they tend to fuck about
Are people who don't have guns.

None of my friends has a machine-gun ready,
Let alone a tank.

A few yards ahead of us, a row of truncheons.
Behind the truncheons, rifles,
Behind the rifles, grenades,
Behind the grenades, machine-guns,
Behind the machine-guns, tanks,
Behind the tanks, bombs,
And behind the bombs — the rich.

The rich are as stupid as guns.
They will be killed with their own guns.

In every capital
The fuckedabout of the world are taking arms.
The people of the world
Want the world.
We are going to take it.